Bush Days

Alexandra Bernard

BookLeaf
Publishing

India | USA | UK

Presentation by *BookLeaf Publishing*

Web: www.bookleafpub.com

E-mail: info@bookleafpub.com

ISBN : 9789357447942

First edition 2021

DEDICATION

To my family, friends and all avid readers

Spring

Blossoming buds and buzzing bees.
Purple pops and sunrise skies.
Hibernation no longer
as the world comes alive.
Petals open wide
welcoming rays of spring air.
Green appears where skeletons once stood,
yellow floods paddocks
where brown once dominated,
pinks and blues and oranges line roads
where grey once lay.
Birds caw,
filling the gap left behind by icy silence.
Animals roam no longer huddled for warmth.
Nature says hello,
and welcome us back
with arms out wide.

Day's End

Melting icecream skies
stretching as far as the eye can see
The sun giving a final hurrah
as day says goodbye and night says hello.

Rolling hills lie beyond
Fields of yellow forming the brick road into
town
Kangaroos skip by
and birds find home.

The wind roars,
the icy breeze seeping into your bones.
A few snaps,
a drink or two
and a creamy brie.

Ending the day
with a view to awe.

The Drive

Out into the bush
up the dirt roads
into nowhere land.
Amongst the barbed wire
and between the crop lined fields.

The cows block your way,
The radio and your phone lose their way.
There's fresh smells of rain
as the hessian clouds roll in.

Thundering rains
and the dust disappears.
Streaming down the windows,
the wipers go mad.

Back into town and your phone finds itself.
Fields are replaced by houses,
barbed wire with Colorbond
and cows with dogs and cats.

A Day to Try Again Tomorrow

Gloomy skies and foggy minds.
The clouds cry and raindrops run down windows
as teardrops run down cheeks.

Energy levels are drained,
Hunger is staying away
and effort has gone and hid.

The spark hasn't stayed lit
from yesterday.
Tomorrow you can try again.

Crops

A world turned yellow
with criss-cross rows of bright crops
filled with buzzing bees

The Fog

Days are less sunshine and greyer,
than the melty icecream skies
on those early mornings with crashing waves.
The starts are harder to find under the fog
and the blackness lingers longer.
The flowers aren't blooming
as the frost creeps in
and the windy chill culls the greenery.
Sight is harder in the spitting rain and the cold
itches.
The sense of safety,
the warmth from the sun that hugs you tight,
is hidden deep beneath the fog.

Vegetables

Fresh seeds finding soil
nourished by water and light
food begins to grow.

Dawn

The sun pokes its head above the distant hills.
The first glow radiates across the plains,
reaching out to every living thing,
its warmth touching every blade of grass,
illuminating every row of canola afar
and casting long morning shadows.

The distant calls of birds and
moos from cows reach your ears,
as the world awakens.
Otherwise silence,
on this early morning.

The air is still,
a fresh spring morning.
On top of a hill you sit,
watching the sun say good morning.
A warming welcome is exactly why
you awoke before the sun even opened its eyes.

The Shadow

It follows you everywhere,
stealing little pieces of you.
It steals your thoughts and throws them out.
It eats them up and spits them out blurrier
and more disconnected than they were before.
It steals your vibrance and dampens it.
 It robs you of your faith in yourself and your
abilities.
It throws everything in the corner under the pile
of books
and discarded nick nacks.
Quashing the shadow is a little harder,
at times you think you've won but it pounces
once again.
You think it's gone but it's become better at
hiding and better at covering its tracks.
 One day you'll be better at sneaking past it,
escaping its clutches and while you'll forever
have to cover your own tracks
 it won't be able to find you.

Sunset

Dusky pinks and blues
a sombre afternoon sky
to welcome the night

Off

Questions fill your ravaged head,
thoughts overflow from your ears
attacking every inch of your brain.
Too many things,
too little time or maybe too much.
You don't know which to ponder,
which to scrunch up and toss away,
or which to keep for later.
Round and round they go,
a never-ending carousel.
Quietening them is another matter,
harder than it sounds.
If only there was an off switch.

Cheers

A bubbling glass
amongst the garden greens.
The last day's rays cutting through the leaves.
A piece of tranquillity,
even when trains rumble by.
A kookaburra finds home,
its laughs a cheers and farewell
to a celebratory day.

Physical Books

Flicking page by page,
the words fly by,
the stories fill your head.
Into a new world you go,
new friends you make,
new memories you hear.
Absorbed into the ink you become,
reading one by one.
Moment by moment somewhere new,
from Germany to Cuba
and Outback Australia
the world is seen through the pages.
A pile so obscenely large
it should surely topple,
you read on,
all consumed.
The physical page turn
the only way for you.

Words

Your favourite thing by far,
how to combine them,
analyse them,
mix them up and spit them out.
Really just a jumble of letters,
arranged differently,
sometimes without meaning.
You read them now,
not always knowing what they're saying.
You listen to them,
sometimes hearing nothing.
But you,
you really like to write them.

All Masked Up

The faces are hidden,
personality is disappearing,
behind a masking cloth.
Yet it keeps us safe,
people are forgetting,
forgetting what friends look like
behind the thing that makes us all look the same.
Dogs cannot read expressions,
Babies cannot either,
the things that keeps us safe
makes some people lost.
The world has dimmed this last year or two,
and the smile that helps to brighten it
is hidden behind the mask.

Jab

That one little prick
now everything can go back
to normal once more.

Man's Best Friend

Cheery eyes and smiling snouts,
scruffy ears and wagging tails.
Puppy eyes staring at you,
waiting for that all loved belly rub.
Bouncing towards you,
with that all consuming look of love
and joy that only a dog looking at its human
can bring.

Family

The people who care for us,
care about us,
care for what we do,
care for who we are.

The people who support us,
support us in every endeavour,
support us even when me make mistakes,
supports us when we're lost.

We do the same for them
and that's what makes us family.

Fire

Fire crackles,
flames dancing over wood.
Charcoal falls and marshmallows roast.
Food cooks and families drink.
Smoke spirals under clear blue skies,
as people find another Sunday to enjoy.

www.ingramcontent.com/pod-product-compliance
Lightning Source LLC
LaVergne TN
LVHW051252200726
843510LV00011B/1821